# The One Command Commands

Commands created by Asara Lovejoy
Photography and book created by Carol Burk, M.Ed.
Copyright©2013 Carol Burk

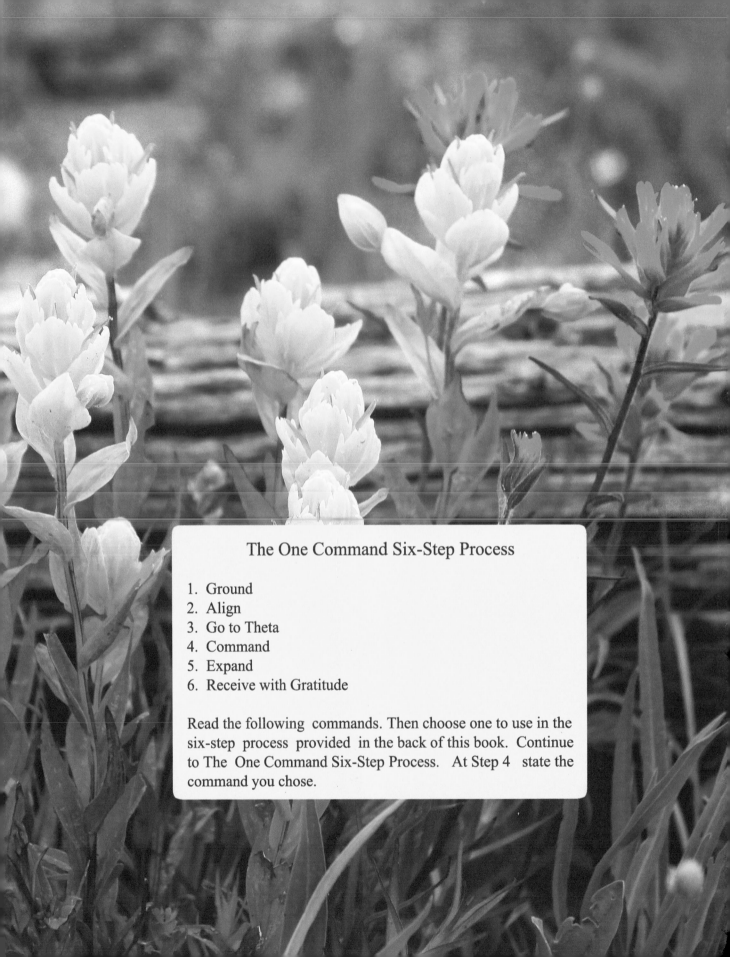

## The One Command Six-Step Process

1. Ground
2. Align
3. Go to Theta
4. Command
5. Expand
6. Receive with Gratitude

Read the following commands. Then choose one to use in the six-step process provided in the back of this book. Continue to The One Command Six-Step Process. At Step 4 state the command you chose.

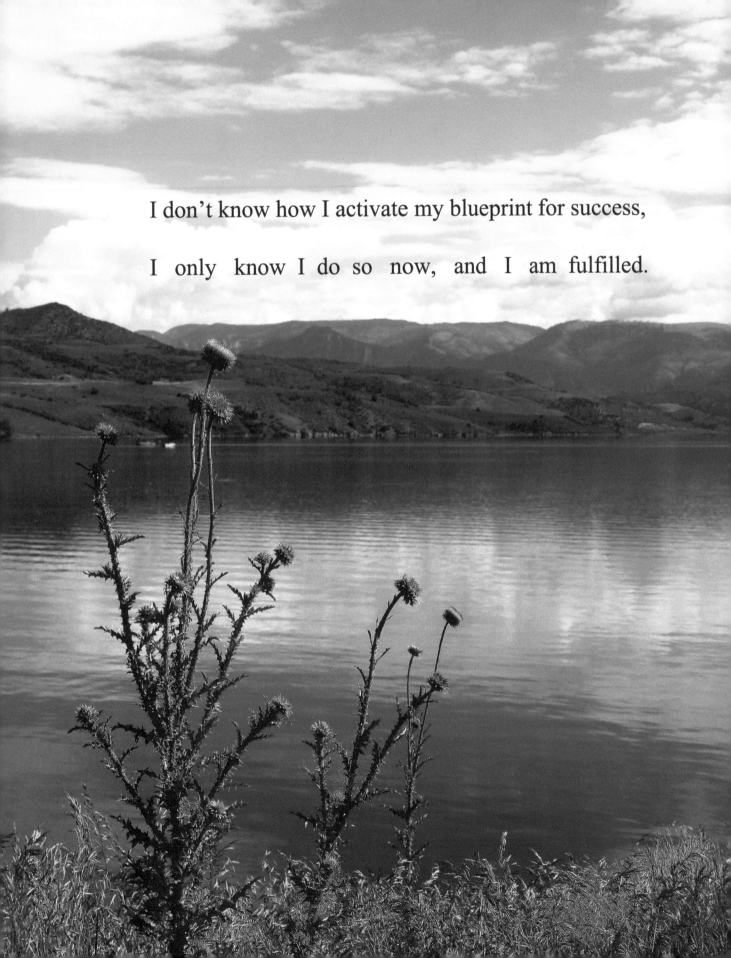

I don't know how I activate my blueprint for success,

I only know I do so now, and I am fulfilled.

I don't know how I am aligned to my true purpose,

I only know I am so now, and I am fulfilled.

I don't know how I allow my genius and intuition to express fully, I only know I do so now, and I am fulfilled.

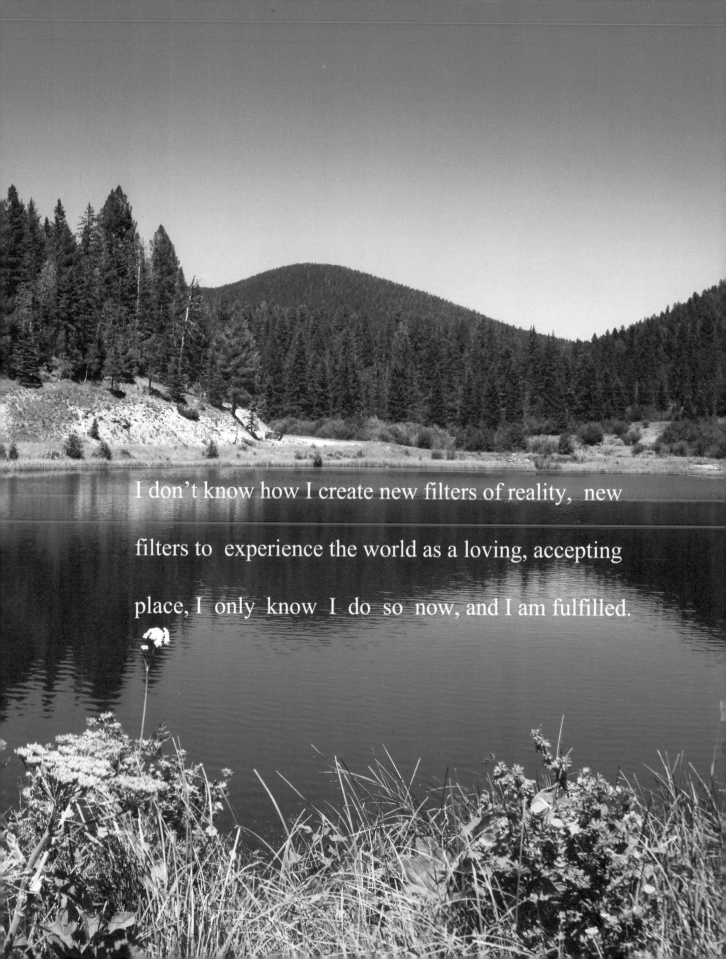

I don't know how I create new filters of reality, new filters to experience the world as a loving, accepting place, I only know I do so now, and I am fulfilled.

I don't know how I come to believe and

know I am the master of my reality,

I only know I do now, and I am fulfilled.

I don't know how I take 100% responsibility for my life, I only know I am free to do so now, and I am responsible.

I don't know how  I enjoy  the freedom of my intelligence  in  new directions, I only know I do so now,  and I celebrate.

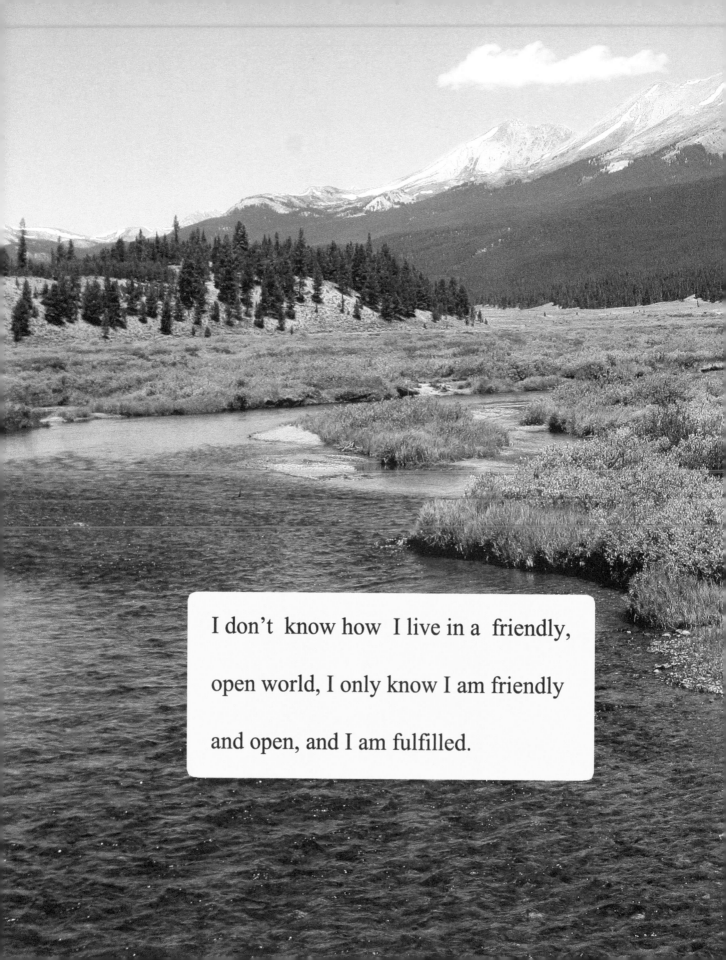

I don't know how I live in a friendly, open world, I only know I am friendly and open, and I am fulfilled.

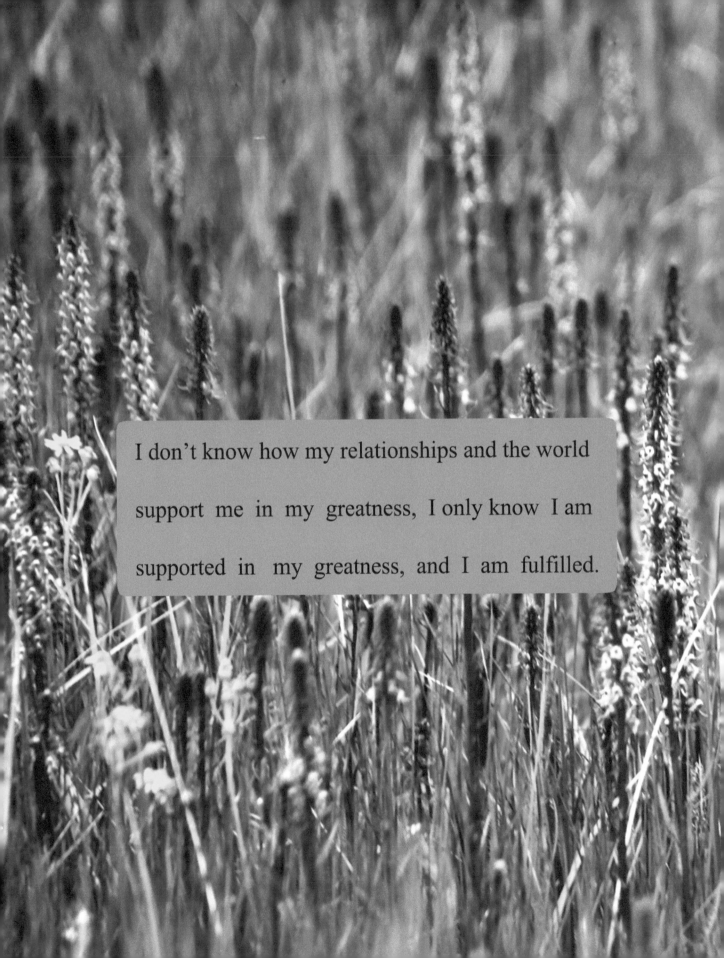

I don't know how my relationships and the world support me in my greatness, I only know I am supported in my greatness, and I am fulfilled.

I don't know how I increase love in my life in all that I do, love within myself, self-love, I only know I do so now, and I am fulfilled.

I don't know how I am so loved and accepted.

I only know I love and accept myself now,

and I am fulfilled.

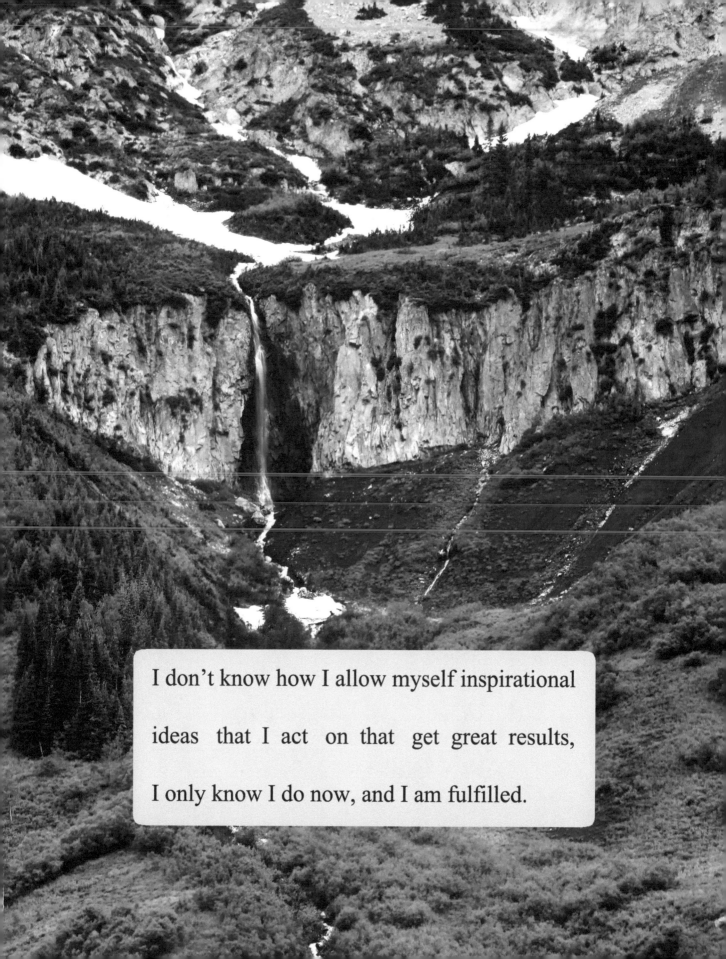

I don't know how I allow myself inspirational ideas that I act on that get great results, I only know I do now, and I am fulfilled.

I don't know how I come to be so courageous, I only know I am courageous now, and I am fulfilled.

I don't know how money flows to me easily now,

I only know I am in the flow of financial freedom

now, and I am fulfilled.

I don't know how dreams come true, I only know

I am a dream come true, and I am fulfilled.

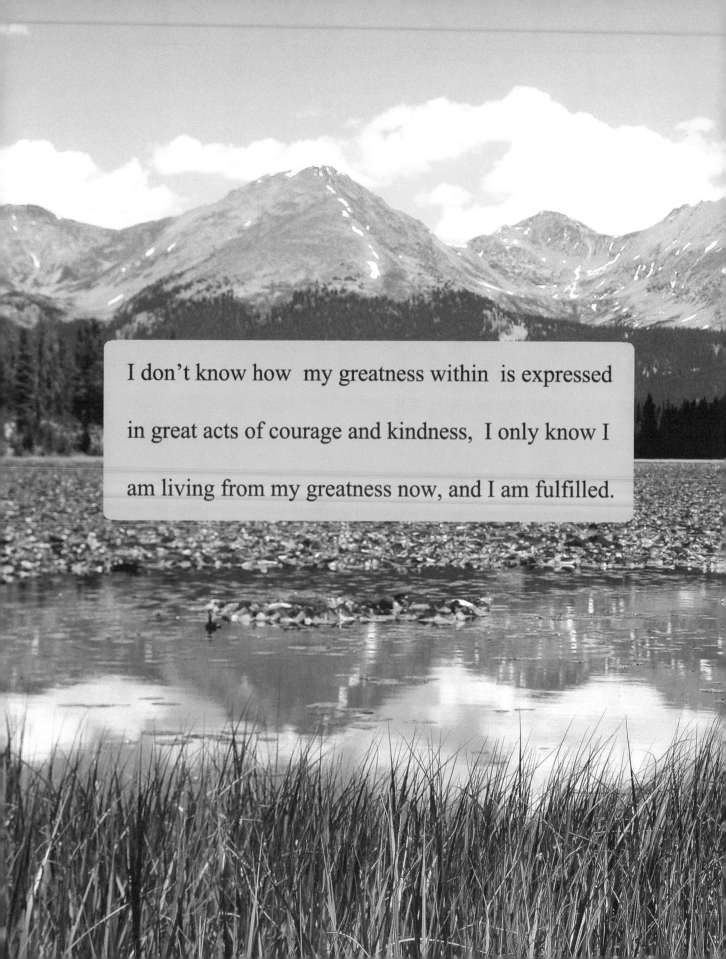

I don't know how  my greatness within  is expressed

in great acts of courage and kindness,  I only know I

am living from my greatness now, and I am fulfilled.

I don't know how I increase my family support,

my devotion to my faith, my support of friends,

I only know I do now, and I am fulfilled.

I don't know how I create an enthusiastic

community of support for me, I only know

I am supported now, and I am fulfilled.

I don't know how I am so healthy and energetic in all the cells of my body, I only know I am now, and I am fulfilled.

I don't know how my mind is clear,

my thoughts are clear, my path is clear,

I only know it is so now, and I am fulfilled.

I don't know how I enjoy nature, the smell of flowers and leaves, and the sun in the trees, I only know I am in relationship with nature now, and I am fulfilled.

I don't know how there is enough time for me, I only know that I make time for myself and my needs, and I am fulfilled.

I don't know how I receive compliments easily and in receiving I am giving, I only know I do so now, and I am fulfilled.

I don't know how I came to have so much fun in my life, I only know I am having a great time, and I am fulfilled.

I don't know how I allow  my sensuality and

sexuality to  be  a part  of  my  everyday life,

I only know it is  so now,  and  I am fulfilled.

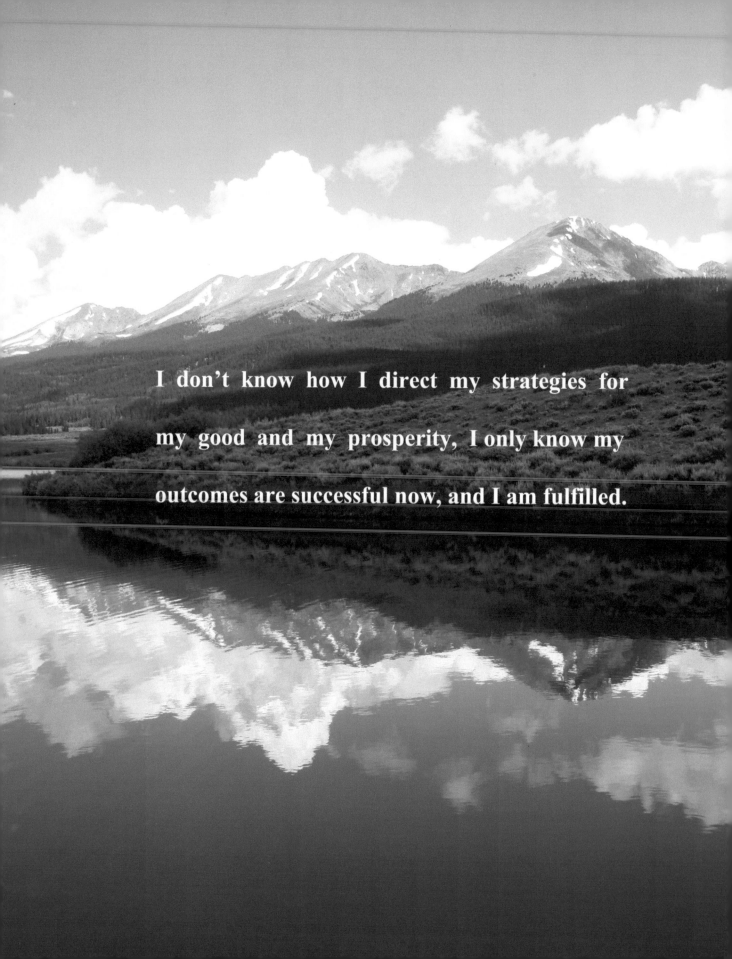

I don't know how I direct my strategies for my good and my prosperity, I only know my outcomes are successful now, and I am fulfilled.

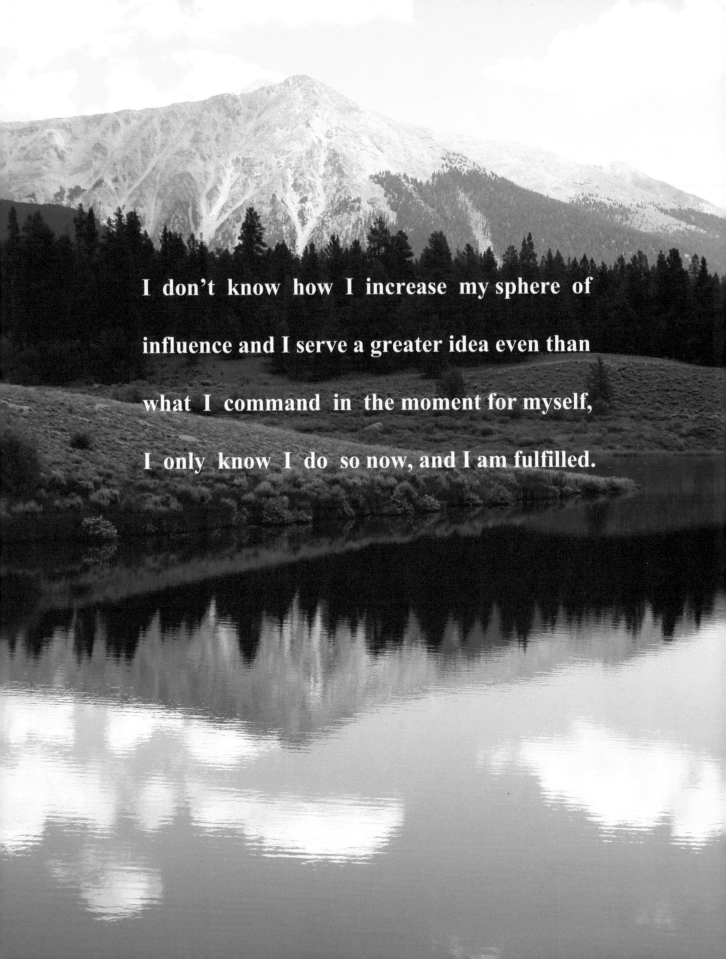

I don't know how I increase my sphere of influence and I serve a greater idea even than what I command in the moment for myself, I only know I do so now, and I am fulfilled.

# The One Command Six-Step Process

1. Ground
2. Align
3. Go to Theta
4. Command
5. Expand
6. Receive with Gratitude

Write each of the above commands on a separate paper and place the six pieces of paper in a horizontal line on the floor. Stand on each piece of paper, and as you do, follow the words as they are read to you. Stay on each step until you complete your experience, taking as much time as you need, then move sideways to the next step.

Before you step on Ground, think of something you wish to manifest in your life: more money, a car, better health, or a relationship. When you choose what you wish to manifest, first simply have the idea of what it is you would like to create for yourself. Now that you have that idea of what it is you would like to manifest, close your eyes and keep your eyes closed during the entire process. When your eyes are closed, you access different portions of your brain than when your eyes are open. You have a deeper experience when you keep your eyes closed.

Have your partner read these directions, slowly at each step, as he or she guides you through the Six-Step Process. Stay at each step as long as it takes until you know that you are ready to continue. You will know, energetically, when you have completed the experience before moving forward.

Step One: Ground

Listen to the sound of my voice, and feel the weight of your body settling down onto the paper under your feet. Imagine you are like a tree with long deep roots, long roots going deep, deep into the earth. Allow these roots to reach down and wrap around rubies, emeralds and diamonds, into the richness of the earth, going even deeper into those hidden springs of refreshing waters. Allow that earth energy to begin to come up through your feet, into your knees, into your hips, right up your spinal column, traveling down through your arms, across your body, that's right, right into your neck, all through your head, into your eyes, close your eyes, look down into your heart, as you align to your purpose and just feel that love in your heart become illuminated as you begin to expand that love. Breathe into that light. Allow that light to be 360 degrees around you. Breathe again. Just breathe into that unconditional love that is in your heart. Breathe out any separation. Breathe in connection. Stay here until you feel your body shift into a well-grounded state.

## Step Two:  Align

When you are ready, move sideways to the second step and stand on Align.  Imagine all that power of the Earth's energy coming into your body, into your heart.  Now take a deep breath, and as you exhale, imagine that the energy is expanding in all directions around you.  The breath of your heart is expanding in all the directions, above and below and around in all directions.  As you exhale, allow that breath to expand in all directions, aligning you with your purpose in a state of unconditional love.  When you feel your body shift, you are ready to continue.

## Step Three:  Go to Theta

Now move sideways to the third step: Go to Theta.  With your eyes closed, look up as if you are trying to look up into the top of your head and imagine a beautiful golden pole of light and just send your consciousness up that pole of light and as you go up you can look down and see your body knowing that you are completely connected to your body.  And as you go up, the higher you go, the faster you go and soon you are moving past the earth's atmosphere beyond the moon, moving past the planets of our solar system, past the Milky Way to the galaxy and beyond and soon you are whizzing past entire universes and as you come to the last star and pass it, you find yourself in the beautiful black void of space.  Just allow yourself to be surrounded by this beautiful velvet blackness and reach out of that blackness and pull it away like a black curtain revealing the luminescent white light of pure potentiality, pure probability and just allow that energy, allow your self to unfurl in this.  Feel yourself adjusting into this beautiful white light place.  This is the place of creation of all that you desire.  Think and feel from this state of consciousness as you activate your DNA, the cells of your body, and your mind to be that master that you are.

## Step Four:  Command

While holding the thought of what you wish to manifest, mentally and silently Command or have your partner read the commands or command you have chosen:  I don't know how I _____, I only know that I do so now, and I am fulfilled.  Take your time to allow this declaration to fulfill itself energetically in your body, before you move to the next step.

## Step Five:  Expand

Now just allow yourself to now expand into that greater field of consciousness, a greater idea than all the commands and allow yourself to be in the super position of the observer of who you are and just notice through all time and space, through all eternity this is the you that is immortal, the creator, the observer, and the experiencer, and that all the wisdom that we have commanded is yours now.  Watch as new, expanded, bigger ideas arrive. Let it become more beautiful and harmonious.  Stay in this process until you know that it is done. Now that you are in this greater state capacity, move to the sixth step.

Immerse and absorb into your DNA the beauty
of our earth and the One Command Commands.

## Step Six: Receive with Gratitude

State in your mind clearly, "Thank you! It is so!" and experience a sense of gratitude and fulfillment emanating from you and coming into you from Source. While in a state of gratitude, gently, kindly, comfortably, see yourself coming back down that pole of light, coming back down into your body, being here physically in your physical structure and allowing yourself to unwind, unwind, unwind, letting go of all the limiting thoughts and ideas that oppose your dreams fulfilled, your success fulfilled, your desires realized. Let it go, let it go, let it go. Rewind, rewind, rewind. Imagine a new holographic image of this life that is your new life replicating itself in every DNA strand of your body, in every organ of your body, in every follicle of your body, and in every particle of emotion in your body and your thinking. Feel it, accept it, and give thanks again. "Thank you! It is done! It is so!"

Take a deep breath and send your energy down into the Earth to firmly reestablish your ground of being. Adjust your energy. Let your body stretch, flex, and move with this new understanding of reality. Take all the time you need to come once again fully awake and alert into your body. Open your eyes and return to the room.

NOTE: If you are doing this process by yourself, you may wish to cite and record some of your ideas, thoughts, and feelings afterwards. If you are doing this process with a friend, then share what you have discovered.

To train yourself in this process, repeat this at least twice the first time you do it. Practice going through the process every day until it becomes so natural for you that you can go through the Six Steps mentally, instantly, any time that you wish to concentrate on what you want to manifest. Practice until this becomes an unconscious internal process.*          *Process and Commands by Asara Lovejoy.

Join www.CommandingWealth.com for information on the Commanding Wealth Seminars, Free Learning Web Section, Weekly Free Teleconferencing and more.

Carol Burk, M.Ed., the creator of this photo book, greatly appreciates Asara Lovejoy and The One Command. Carol leads groups using The One Command process to create health and prosperity. Before Carol became familiar with The One Command, she wrote a book to help students to learn to love school. Now she has integrated The One Command into the love school program, called "How Can I Love School Today?", to teach students how to take responsibility for their learning and life. The One Command Commands book was written to further help groups and individuals to use this wonderful six- step process.